Madhavi Veronika Broszinski

Angels' messages - In the light of love

Messages from the angels for YOU

Bibliografische Information der Deutschen Nationalbibliothek:
Die Deutsche Nationalbibliothek verzeichnet
diese Publikation in der Deutschen
Nationalbibliografie; detaillierte bibliografische Daten
sind im Internet über http://dnb.dnb.de abrufbar.

© *2018 Madhavi Veronika Broszinski*

Pictures:
Private - Madhavi Veronika Broszinski

Book-Cover:
Lektorat Buchstabenpuzzle
Bianca Karwatt

Text: Madhavi Veronika Broszinski
www.herz-balance.com

Book-Layout:
Lektorat Buchstabenpuzzle
Bianca Karwatt
www.buchstabenpuzzle.de

Translation: Nicole Böer

1. Auflage

Herstellung und Verlag: BoD – Books
on Demand, Norderstedt

ISBN: 978-3-7528-6182-2

Madhavi Veronika Broszinski

Angels' messages - In the light of love

Messages from the angels for YOU

FSC
www.fsc.org

MIX

Papier aus ver-
antwortungsvollen
Quellen

Paper from
responsible sources

FSC® C105338

Inhalt

Preface

In this book you can read many little sayings and affirmations. Positive thinking can help you get over things, especially things in the negative realm of life. Crises, losses of beloved people or pets, bullying at work, illnesses and permanent stress are only a few examples of what can throw us off balance. This is exactly why it is important to use the positive things of life to regain stability, strength, courage and new ideas. Following new paths means leaving old things behind.

With this book I want to give you all an accompaniment which might be your friend in allowing your life to change in a great way.

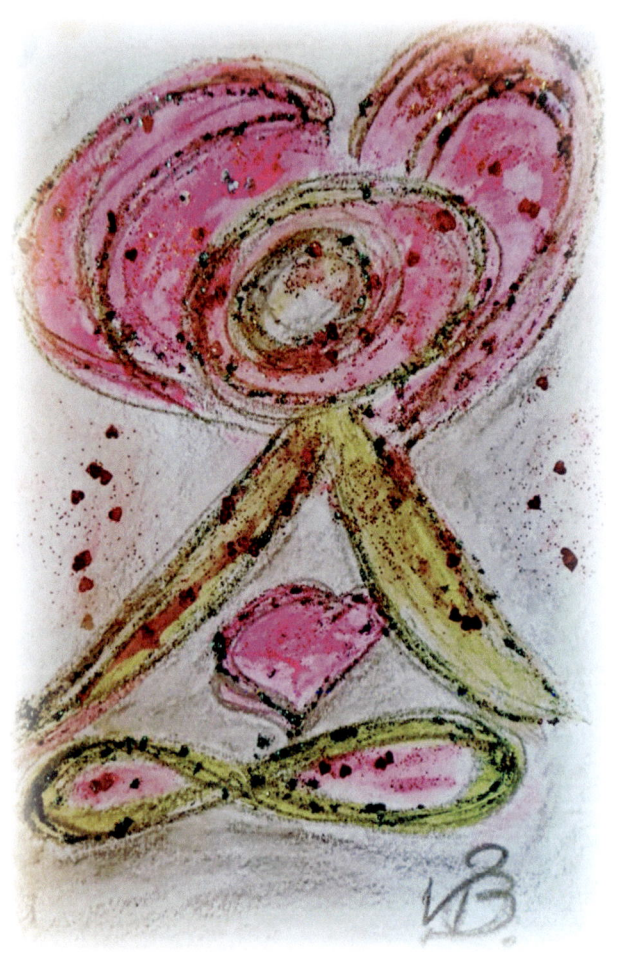

About this book

This little book enables you to choose and read the angels' messages at any time. That way you can make use of their affirmative character for your very own motivation.

All the little angelic poems are positive and combined with angel pictures. Soon the book will make you feel that your little angel is right beside you.

The path is leading in positiveness so that EVERYONE can get a portion of luck, happiness and energy into their hands. That way, everyone can withstand all kinds of crises and losses.

The pictures will give you the shine and colors from the light of LOVE. Let the energies of the angels enchant you. Happiness and love is your omnipresent companion.

The angels do have a word for all human beings and it is able to touch you. This word is called LOVE.

I dedicate this book to my
children and grandchildren.

Messages for you to
create a better perception

No matter what happens, no matter which injuries bother you, there is always a solution to arrive at and be with yourself. Listen to your heart with all its calm and depth. Happiness calls this place home. And you deserve to enjoy all this happiness sponsored by the sparkling energy of your angels.

That way the angels want to show you how to manage the situation which is bothering you. Us, the angels, are there for EVERYONE - big and small, but also happy and unhappy. The only thing you have to do is to take time for YOURSELF. But you need to be brave. That is what you can use our energy for. This energy lies within these texts and pictures which you are reading and looking at in this very moment. The angels will hand you the necessary tools for the realization of your plans.

The most important message is: »You are the creator of your life.«

The angels are there for you. Your task is to let them know when you need their help. Just tell them!

This is possible with a little prayer: »I ask my guardian angels for love, mercy and healing for myself. That it is, Amen!« You can say this little prayer every morning or evening and repeat it three times.

You'll have a result in no time. Try it! The angels are always ready for you!

The angels have another message for you. It is about the calm in you. Here you can try out something totally new. The angels' magic word is »Meditation«. No matter how you start your meditation, it will provide you with inner peace and calmness which you need to receive new stimuli for yourself.

The way of meditating is very easy, everyone can do it. Close your eyes and breathe in and out through your nose. When you are relaxed and calm you can let go off all old stuff. At the same time you will feel warm and fuzzy inside.

A guided meditation or music accompaniment is another way to feel your inner calm. Try it! We angels are always with you!

These little exercises can be applied by anyone who allows them. When applying the little prayer to the angels combined with the meditation, you will find inner contentedness and love. Yes, love towards yourself and to every thing being.

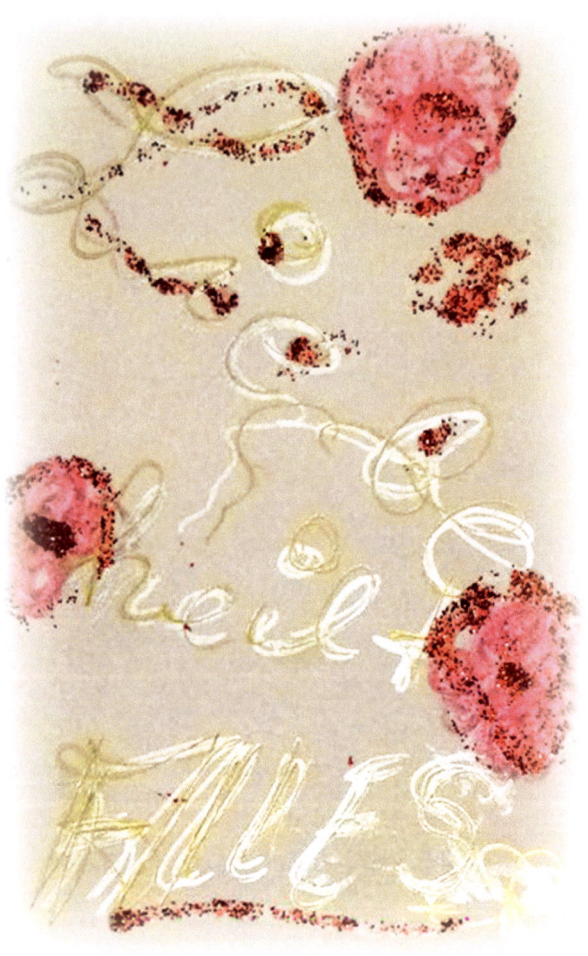

Pictures of love

LOVE

Tolerance and acceptance is unconditional love. Love from your inner self to yourself and everything being.

Positive things

Do good things for yourself and others. The positive things are the things that bring good luck.

Thoughts for the evening

Create your life by yourself. You will get anything you could wish for as soon as you are ready to lead your thoughts towards positiveness.

Trust life

It is the light which enlightens.
It is love which heals.
It is life which is wonderful in so far you trust your intuition.
Hope, love and trust - that is what carries you on in LIFE.

Peace

Peace within ourselves takes us to places where we are supposed to be. That is where our attention leads to and that is where our energy flows.

Open your heart

Open your hearts for the love of yourself and others. It is vital to open your heart. Only love can heal.

All we are looking for

You are the flower of life. Take a look INSIDE you, there you will find everything you have been looking for outside of you.

Trust in yourselves

Trust yourselves and regain your strength from inside you. That makes you authentic and you can live according to your inner calling.
Listen to your inward voice and go your own way.

Understanding

Please look inside you and detect how much understanding you have for the things you do every day. That way you will come to understand step by step that other people also do their things their way. It is about learning to tolerate and sympathize with oneself and others.

Successful

Success depends on how you are INSIDE you. Thinking positively, speaking positively and acting positively creates positive matter.

Meekness and Love

Living in meekness and love in your BEING is the greatest good we may achieve.

Expanding your consciousness

Conscious being means living at the moment, right here and now. That way we get the chance to feel ourselves in one piece and to create a connection between heaven and earth.

Perception and Intuition

Your inner perception is based on a trained intuition. It is most important for your being to accept this intuition. Meditation is a good opportunity to feel and expand our perception.

Generosity

Open your hearts for LOVE. It is the love on earth which heals anything that exists. Love is the only supporting power.
A great heart full of love lives within the hearts of all people. Let the love out with all its generosity.

Meditation

You need inner calmness to master everyday-life.
You need inner calmness to get access to yourself.
You need inner calmness to become one with your soul.
That is what is significant about meditation - arriving here and now in ourselves.

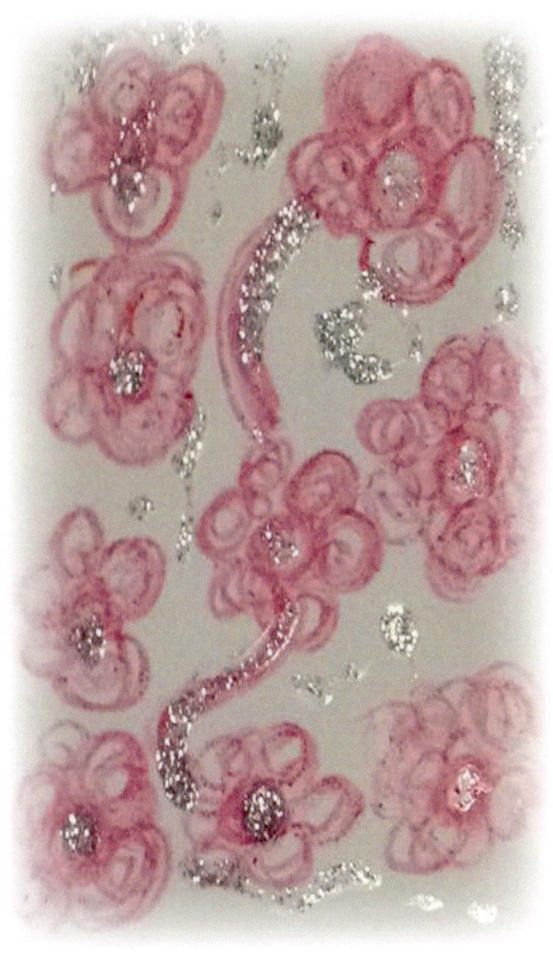

What your angels want to forward to you

These little poems, which you are going to read right here, are presents for you from the angels. Enjoy life in all its shades. Use love to live in this bipolar world. You will have to learn to accept the good and bad sides of life. That way you are always capable of taking in the best and producing the best from it.

Patience

Patience is the only thing which tests us in multiple ways. But at the same time it resolves deep problems and wonderful things can develop.

Strength is born of Calmness

When calm and silent, we are able to make decisions. By listening into ourselves, we can manage to decide from within.

By this our body and mind is in calmness. So our heart does decide. Consequently we are capable of dealing in the outside from the inside.

Experiences

All experiences come from the here and now. So it is vital to accept them. They make the sense in our lives, no matter which direction they are leading to. This is vividly experiencing. Don't get mislead into the past or the future, stay here, in the present.

Emptiness

Only when we are empty on the inside, we will be able to get filled again. This reciprocity between emptiness and denseness appears within us. Still meditation is the origin of NEW developments.

The mirror discloses who we are

Quote of the Day

Not before our heart is not pure and great, the mirror will begin to disclose to ourselves our true face. You are unique, you are loved and you are the one that can manage to accomplish great things.

Our INSIDE shows us the way

A lot of things look different from the OUTSIDE than from the INSIDE. Because of that our HEART guides us the way. You need CALMNESS in your heart on the one hand and your pure thoughts on the other hand. Only positive thoughts will trigger changes that are useful to us.

Trust

Trust in yourself and in everything else is the basis of great love.
That goes along with your sense of responsibility to take responsibility for yourself - and acting it out with the help of the angels' power.
Let's feel into our hearts - there is the golden key.
Are we courageous enough to see what the golden key shows us?
That is what everybody has within him- or herself.
Disover the golden key for yourself and use it.
This aim in view, I wish you a nice evening. The golden key shows where the treasures are hidden.
With LOVE from deep in my heart.

Twinkling stars

The twinkling stars accompany you along your way. Children and yourself are just like the twinkling - LOVE bears ANYTHING.

The inner child

Children are delicate plants. They want to be nourished and cherished. Be like a CHILD! Get to know your inner child.

»The angels accompany you all - ALWAYS. All of us can sense them, as soon as we open our hearts.«

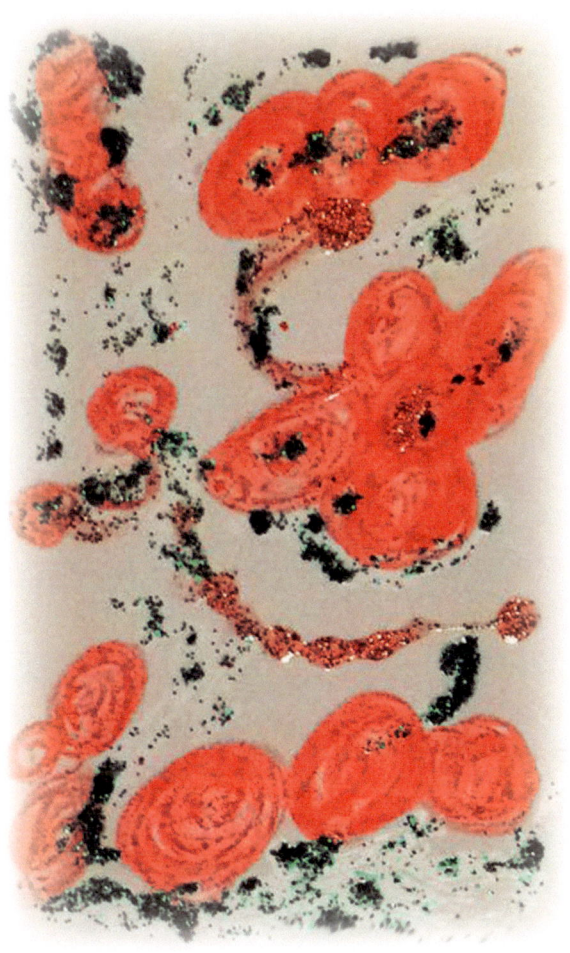

The short ways to yourself

Sometimes we are left alone with our destiny. There is a lot that we do not understand or do not want to realize. But there is always a LIGHT at the end of the tunnel. That is the light the angels want to point at.

That for they tell us this story:

»A little girl called Claudia wanted to visit her grandma during the school holidays in autumn. But things turned out differently. Grandma had to get surgery in hospital. She had to stay there for some weeks to get better. When granny woke up after anaesthesia she recognized a clear voice. This voice uttered: »Don't worry, my dear, everything happens according to the angels' planning.« Grandma was totally surprised that the angels were talking to her, though she had always been about to talk to them. Unfortunately life was busy and there was always a reason to postpone the talks to later. Finally the ‚later' was ‚now' and she listened what the angels had to say. »The cards that you use for your work with people are very important tools. You will see that you will be able to read more and more from them.« Granny was glad about this message because she helped and supported other people by using those cards. Exactly these cards were very special.

Each card showed different angels in different sizes and colors - each with a different story to tell. She had learned to use her impulses for converting their information into the present situation. While lying in bed after surgery, grandma was in a state of deep calmness and had no difficulty to realize what the angels were saying. She applied later on what she had heard.

Her granddaughter came to visit the next day. She was relieved to see her grandma getting better and soon she learned about grandma's talk to the angels.

Claudia was all ears, as it is easy for her to perceive the presence of angels in her everyday life. Claudia meditated a lot, as she needed it to switch off the stress in daily life. This way of relaxing was taught to her in afternoon classes in the private school that she attended.

Claudia could tell her grandma so many things she saw or felt in her meditations. Once there was a strange situation in a still meditation. She told her grandma about it when she visited her in hospital.

»You know, granny, I formed a habit of meditating every day when I get back home from school. I enjoy a short break and silence. One time I was able to see lots of colors. It was like a colorful rainbow. At one side of the rainbow there was a white and purple angel who winked at me and said: ›Claudia, this is exactly the right way you have chosen to find more calmness for yourself.‹« Grandma padded Claudia's hair. »You are right, my child, you have already learned how to relax. Like this it is easy for you to regain strength for studying.«

Claudia speaks a lot about her perceptions in meditation when grandma is around. She is quick in recognizing, sensing and hearing things that she can use for her everyday life.

In her school Claudia spoke about her own relaxation-project. Now the children and adults also make use of it. Both teachers and educators have learned to relax in a short time on short paths.

The advantages are convincing. Concentration is easy to maintain when calm and so there is enough energy available for our school and work life.

Little helpers for everyday-life

We, the angels, have thought about how we can support you all with little helpers. These little helpers are little things which can brighten up your day. That way everybody can concentrate their energies to an optimum in order to transform their negative moments. EVERYONE can overcome blocked experiences. Your thoughts are like a little seed that has to be sown to be able to create POSITIVENESS. Whatever people think, they also pronounce. Whatever is pronounced, will be transformed into matter. As a result, as soon as you start thinking, the outcome has already been created. Accordingly, positive thinking, speaking and acting implicitly creates positive outcomes.

There are so many things in life which make us happy. Nature provides us with plants, flowers and animals, but also with clean oxygen in the forests. All of those are little helpers, which are good for us. Anyway, there is more of this. For instance positive, affirming angel messages can help us with a good start into the day. As well as angel pictures may warm our hearts. A positive effect on our perception can be produced by healing stones or maybe the pleasant smell of an essential oil.

It's the little things which make us great. The little helpers can help us to manage the transformation of negative events in our life.

The first step of creating something new depends on each single one of us. Be courageous enough to go into yourself and listen to the positive signs in your life. Accept the love from your inner heart as the key to your insight.

**LOVE is the only healing
and supporting power!**

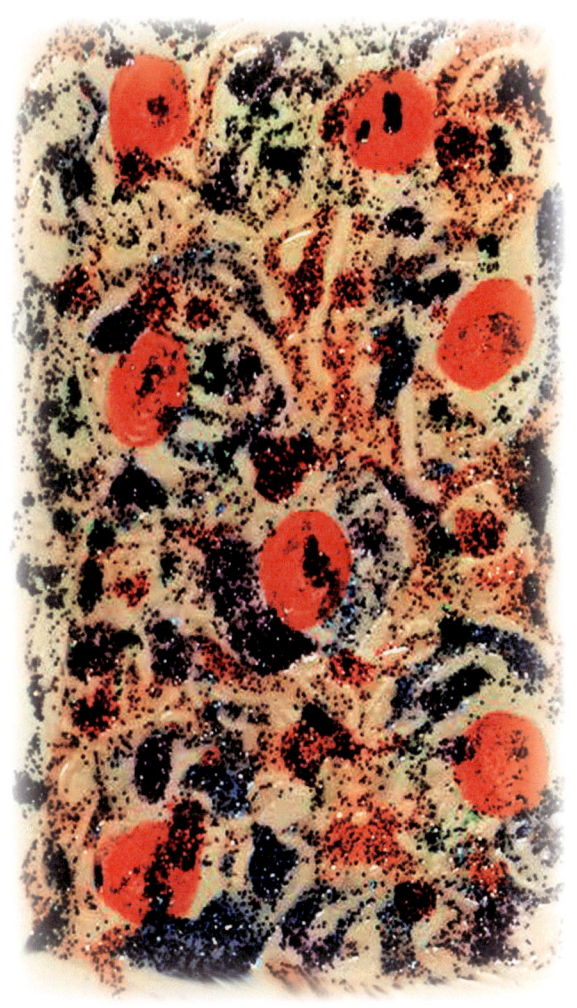

Accepting happiness and love

Accepting happiness and love is for some people a big challenge in life. Many people are not aware of how they block things in life by behaving the way they do.

So the angels want to tell a story for everyone who had a dream at some point in their lives.

In dream wonderland a woman called Maria realized in what situation she has found herself. She travelled to a far place and discovered there many spices she had not known before. Maria had never before seen those spices - chili, curcuma and cinnamon - where they actually grow. The colors and smells were so enticing for Maria. In this dream she grew the spices on her very own plantation and she knew exactly which spice was to be used for which dish. But at work she knew another way how to use the spices. She worked as a massage therapist in a therapy center. Many people who suffered from burnout came to see her there. They had also booked massages for relaxing, which they could enjoy long-term. Pure organic herbal oils were applied in the massages, as well as special thermal massages with cinnamon spices. In this dream she could also see another professional field for herself. She treated her clients with energetic healing and was very successful in it. She also wrote books about holistic ways of how to lead people to self healing. In this dream Maria was a very successful woman with an incredibly big store of knowledge. When Maria woke up in the morning, she was so cheerful and delighted by the dream that she immediately began writing down what she saw in her dream. She herself has been a mobbing target for quite a while and did not know what to do.

This dream was just about right. Maria started reading about holistic healing and enjoyed trainings in many fields the following year. After five years of training and treating clients she could be proud of how she had succeeded so far.

What was her secret?
She has used the power of the dream. Her soul showed her the way. Our soul uses dreams to show us what we can do.

Be brave enough to look at what the soul shows to you. The access is via your dreams or your daily meditations.

Love is in ALL of it!

Exploring new ways peacefully

This chapter will give you another chance to read about angels' wonderful recommendations for all of us.

There is always the good, which helps you to set a new focus in your life. Every little step provides you with power and energy to go your own way step by step. That is why the angels keep these little presents available for you.

Inner happiness is the light to see the love of what can be offered to you. In every little detail you can see what your perception means to unclose to you.

Take over the viewpoint of a child. Children's eyes are pure, they love unconditionally. They give love from within. There is positiveness in every single thing and one of us. Be ready to discover it - within yourself and within others. Everything you detect as something positive in others, is part of your own positiveness. There is always light and shadow in every single situation and person. That is why there is only one power - the LOVE. Root LOVE in your hearts - it will bring you inner peace, which is part of you anyway.

This power is rooted in the hearts of mankind, all around the world. The key to open this door is included in everyone. Be brave enough to use your key to open your hearts. The peace on all paths belongs to each one of you.

Life is worth living - also for YOU!

Postface

These stories, pictures and affirmations are carried by the energy of the angels. The angels are always around us and wait to be asked to be allowed to help you.

We are prepared to assist you whenever you need us to. Be courageous to speak to us in calmness and love.

All happiness lies within your hearts.

Acknowledgements by the author

I want to use the chance to say thank you to the people who supported me with this book.

I express my deepest thanks to my lovely husband Bernd who gave me all his support and many ideas on producing this book.

I give my sincere thanks to my parents because they taught me to pursue and fulfill my paths and aims.

A big thank you I want to pronounce for Bianca Karwatt. With her help and support I managed to create this cover within love to everything, as well as the layout of the book as a total.

I give my thanks to all my teachers, who did and will keep on accompanying me on my way.

So nah und doch so fern

About the author

Madhavi Veronika Broszinski is a trained Hatha Yoga teacher (BYV), Children Yoga teacher (BYV), and Bhakti Yoga teacher.

She was trained according to the teachings of Sivananda in Hatha Yoga in the Yoga Vidya Training Center - Bad Meinberg.

She got the holistic practice and holistic view through different living conditions.
Madhavi Veronika Broszinski completed her training in Ayurveda and Ayurvedic massage in Sri Lanka.

In her seminars she trains with a lot of love - from her own life experiences and spiritual experiences.

Her heart beats for Bhakti Yoga and Mantra chanting. The spirituality shows itself in her books in word and writing and via her soul painting.

India and Sri Lanka are reflected in her work. Since

2009, she has been working in her calling in her own practice.

She created the Rainbow Light Coaching system. That way she can get to connect in the deep spiritual levels. She connected the power of colors with the teaching of the Chakras.

Madhavi Veronika Broszinski is married. She has two grown children and seven grandchildren.

Contact

I am at your disposal for individual consultation anytime and anywhere.

You can see my lectures, seminars, workshops and retreats and more information at www.herz-balance.com.

Weitere Bücher
der Autorin

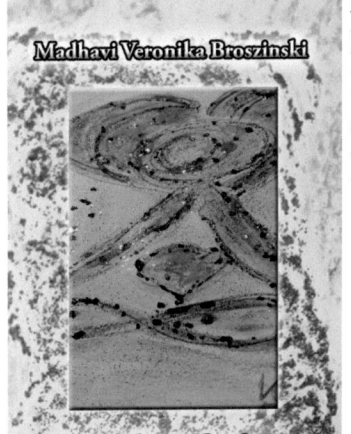

Engelsbotschaften
Im Licht der Liebe
Paperback
60 Seiten, 9,99 €
ISBN 9783746033211

Angels' messages
In the light of love
Paperback
56 Seiten, 9,99 €
ISBN 9783752861822

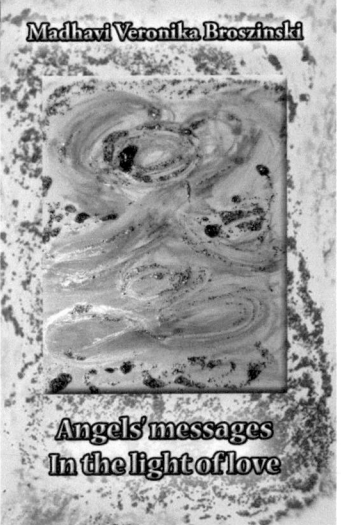

Fantasiereisen erleben und fühlen
Paperback
64 Seiten, 9,99 €
ISBN 9783753496504

Meine Schwester, der Engel auf Erden
Paperback
120 Seiten, 6,00 €
ISBN 9783744897655

For your personal notes

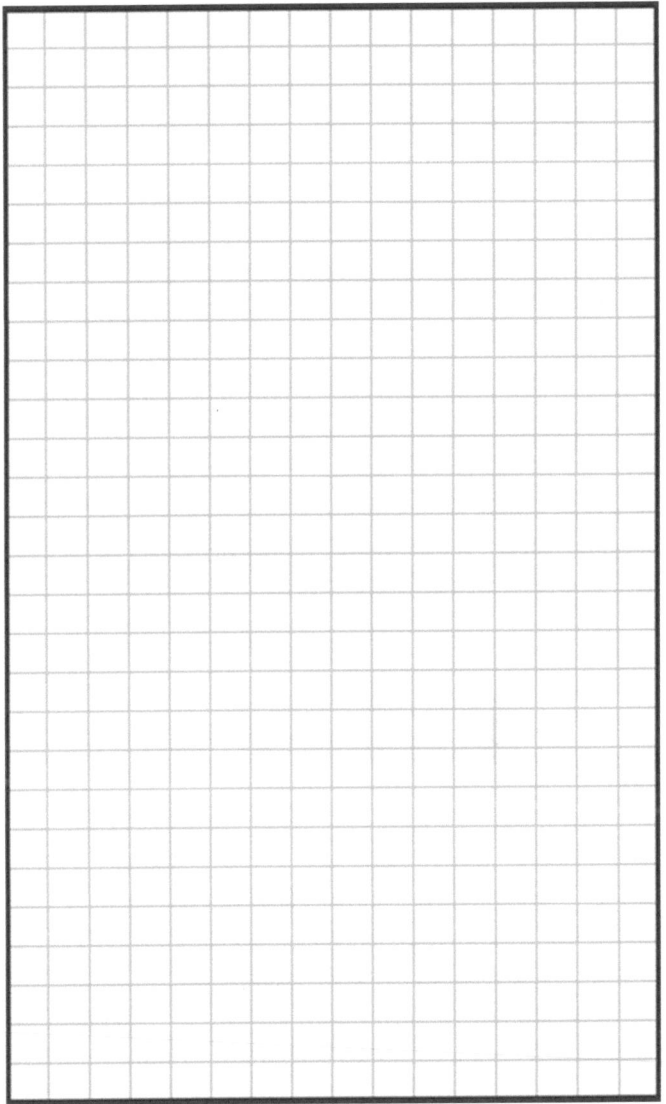

53